A Place to Belong

Debbie Friedman
Sings Her Way Home

by Deborah Lakritz
illustrated by Julia Castaño

APPLES & HONEY PRESS

To Freda z"l, Cheryl, and Amy for
trusting me and telling the stories. -DL

To Bonnie, Lulu, Michiru, and the Monkey.
You are where I belong. -JC

Apples & Honey Press
An Imprint of Behrman House Publishers
Millburn, New Jersey 07041
www.applesandhoneypress.com

ISBN: 978-1-68115-610-1

Library of Congress Cataloging-in-Publication Data

Names: Lakritz, Deborah, author. | Castaño, Julia, illustrator.
Title: A place to belong : Debbie Friedman sings her way home / by Deborah
   Lakritz ; illustrated by Julia Castaño.
Description: Millburn, New Jersey : Apples & Honey Press, 2022. | Summary:
   "A lyrical, uplifting story about how Debbie Friedman got her start as a
   musician"–Provided by publisher.
Identifiers: LCCN 2022019101 | ISBN 9781681156101 (hardcover)
Subjects: LCSH: Friedman, Debbie–Juvenile literature. | Jewish

Design by Alexandra N. Segal
Edited by Alef Davis
Art Directed by Ann Koffsky
Printed in the United States

9 8 7 6 5 4 3 2 1

Debbie waits beside gleaming candlesticks.
Bubbie and Zayde hurry downstairs. Aunts, uncles,
and cousins arrive just in time.

Hiss goes Bubbie's match as it
touches flickering flame to candles.
Debbie snuggles close. They whisper
the blessing together.

"Good Shabbos!"

The room overflows with chatter.
Hugs. The heavenly smell of Mother's brisket.

Laughter at Debbie's jokes and comical expressions.

And joy, always, at her sweet singing.

Debbie's Jewish life in Utica, New York, is full.
This is where she belongs.

But Father wants a change. One day he announces,
"We're moving to Minnesota. To a new life!"
Debbie clings to Bubbie. She doesn't want to go.

Saint Paul is lonely. No laughing with aunts, uncles,
and cousins. No lighting candles with Bubbie.
Debbie wonders, *Will I ever belong?*

Maybe Hebrew school will help. "Please send me!"
she begs her parents. They say yes.

In class, Debbie's teacher calls her
Dinaleh, for her Hebrew name, Dinah.
He teaches her the Sh'ma and V'ahavta—
prayers that connect the Jewish people to God.

Shabbat mornings, Debbie walks to junior congregation.
Hebrew prayers sail from her lips, and her chest fills
with a warm glow.

But once she is a teenager, Debbie moves to adult services.
Disappointment wedges into her heart.

Services are

solemn,

serious,

boring.

The cantor and choir sing. The congregation listens.
Debbie thinks, *What am I doing here? I'll never belong.*

Still searching for her place, sixteen-year-old Debbie snags
a babysitting job at a Jewish sleepaway camp. It's 1967.
Everyone sings about love, peace, and freedom.
Things that matter to people's hearts.

A campfire beckons her one evening. Campers and counselors
sing. Debbie's soul stirs, and her own voice rises to join in.
The songs aren't Jewish but they feel like prayers.

The next day Debbie begs a counselor to teach her some chords. Steel strings jab at her tender fingers. She ignores the pain and learns fast. More than anything, she longs to buy her *own* guitar.

Back home, Debbie juggles jobs:

salad girl,

dishwasher,

short-order cook.

Until, at last, she has the money she needs.

Stretching her arms around her shiny new instrument, Debbie learns the folk songs from camp. Day and night she practices until her fingers are raw. Soon music dances from her fingertips and sails from her lips.

It's time to show her youth group!
"Play us a song," her friends say.

Her voice soars with passion. Her eyes sparkle with life.
Everyone cheers.

"We need you," synagogue directors say. "Be our song leader!"
Youth groups cram into living rooms and basements for
Debbie's sing-alongs, and she teaches them folk songs by
popular musicians of the day.

"C'mon, people in the back!" she jokes. Debbie uses silly faces
and funny voices to make the shyest people feel like they
belong too.

Debbie is eager for more. Soon she is crisscrossing the country, folk tunes ready and guitar in hand.

"**Louder!**" she coaxes children at Jewish summer camps.

"**Again!**" she cheers on teens at youth retreats.

"**Beautiful!**" she praises congregations at Shabbat services.

But something nags at Debbie. *Where are the Jewish songs that speak to our hearts?*

One day on the bus, Debbie watches the world go by.
What about me? she thinks, loneliness tugging at her.
Where am I going?

In the quiet of her heart a melody grows, soothing and tender. She joins it with the English translation of the V'ahavta, a prayer she's treasured since Hebrew school. It describes loving God and instilling that love in your children. Debbie holds the song deep in her soul.

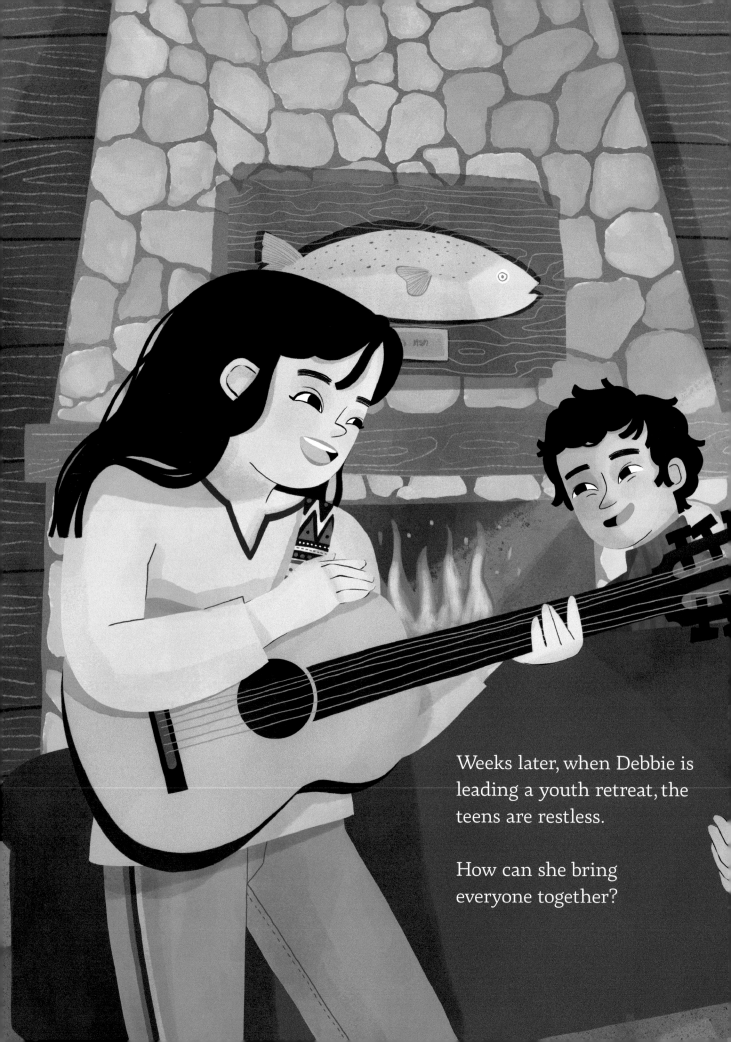

Weeks later, when Debbie is leading a youth retreat, the teens are restless.

How can she bring everyone together?

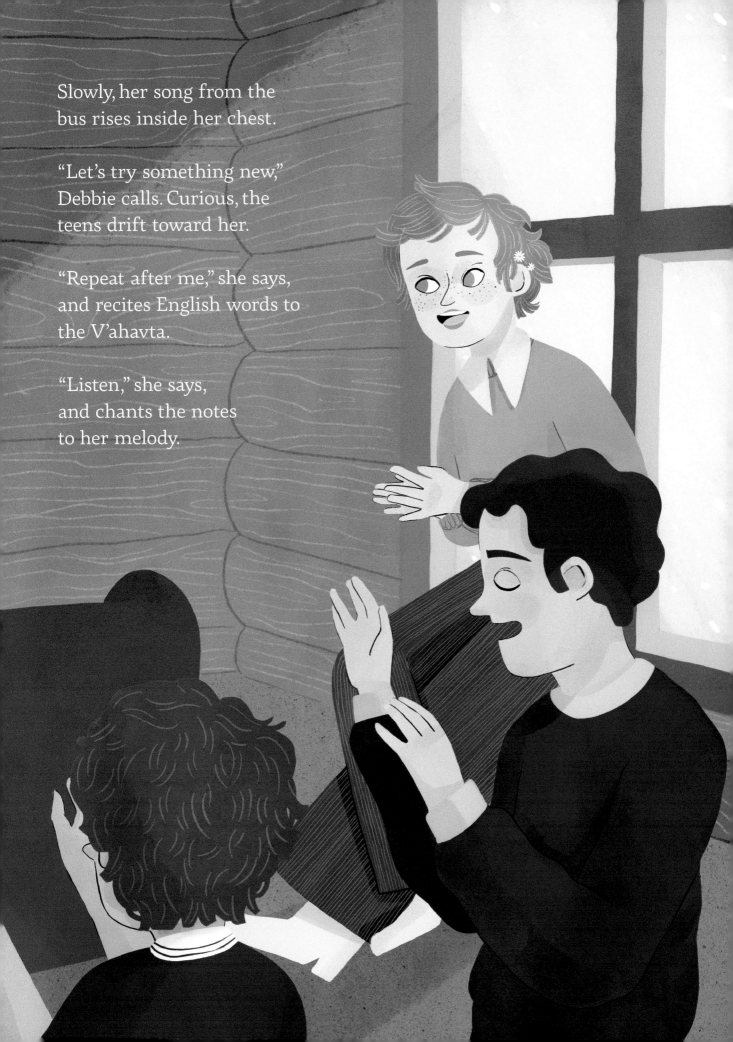

Slowly, her song from the
bus rises inside her chest.

"Let's try something new,"
Debbie calls. Curious, the
teens drift toward her.

"Repeat after me," she says,
and recites English words to
the V'ahavta.

"Listen," she says,
and chants the notes
to her melody.

The teens stumble at first. But once they echo her, something amazing happens.

As they sing, the teens put their arms around one another. For the first time, the prayer belongs to them, not to a cantor or choir. It's as if light suddenly shines on a road that Debbie never knew existed.

This bright new road
leads her to Jews of
all backgrounds—

**TRADITIONAL, MODERN,
young, old,**

those who feel connected to Jewish life,
and those who have felt forgotten.

They all find a home in her music:
A lively "Oseh Shalom" for peace.
A jubilant "Miriam's Song" to honor women.
An emotional "Mi Shebeirach" for those who seek healing.
Crowds sing her songs arm in arm, with full hearts.

And as her music becomes a part of them, they teach it to their children, who teach it to their children.

Now Debbie's music belongs to the world.

And she does too.

A Note for Families

We've all had the experience of creating something
new and uniquely ours. The spark of an idea may become
a painting full of lively colors. A magical story. A dance full of
twirls and sways. A towering structure made of Legos.

"I must do this!" the spark says to you.

But where does this spark come from?

Our creativity begins deep inside us. Our ideas grow from a mixture of
everything we experience in our lives: the love we give and receive, our
memories, the beauty of nature, our everyday activities, and a bit of the
unknown.

Sometimes our creativity can even come from sadness, or a wish for things
to change.

Debbie Friedman's music came from many places: her joy in being Jewish,
the warmth she felt in singing with others, and a loneliness she yearned to
fill. She often said her musical talent and creativity were gifts, blessings she
was forever grateful to have received and, more importantly, to share.

When Debbie shared her talents, first with her own community and then
with the greater Jewish world, she opened up a sacred space—
a place where others felt like they finally belonged and a place Debbie had
been searching for too.

What are your gifts?

How can you use your creativity to bring joy and meaning
into your life and the lives of those around you?

I invite you to honor this holy part of yourself and share it with others!

Wishing you sparks,

Deborah